# From Passion to Profit:
## *A Complete Guide to Creating and Marketing Your Photography Business*

AMANDA OTIS

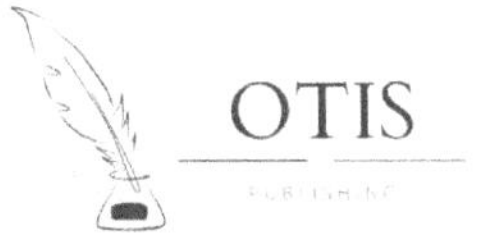

OTIS

# Contents

# Introduction

Imagine the scene: You've just concluded a breathtaking photo shoot. The natural light was enchanting, your subject radiated joy, and the resulting images are of such exceptional quality that you can't help but envision the resounding accolades they will garner.

But before you get lost in social media validation, let's channel creative inspiration into laying the groundwork for your photography business. Even the most artistically inclined among us must venture into the essential details of business to transform our passion into a sustainable and prosperous venture. Let's discover how to elevate your photography hobby into a thriving and rewarding industry.

# Chapter 1: Setting Up Your Photography Business

Photography Business Registration and Legalities

First things first, let's talk legality. Registering your photography business might sound as dry as day-old toast, but it's essential. You wouldn't drive a car without registering it. Similarly, you'll need to register your business to give it legitimacy and protect your assets from business liabilities. The process involves registering your business name, obtaining necessary permits and licenses, and ensuring compliance with local regulations. Check with your local city hall or a business advisor for specific requirements. Each area has its own set of rules, and you want to ensure you're following them.

Choosing a Business Structure

Next, you'll need to choose a business structure. If you're working solo, consider a Sole Proprietorship. If you have a business partner, a Partnership might suit you. You could opt for an LLC (Limited Liability Company) for added liability protection. Each structure has different tax implications and affects your role within your company, so it's essential to choose wisely.

Setting Up a Home Studio vs. Renting Space

Deciding where to set up your photography business is the next step. Transforming a part of your home into a studio is budget- friendly and convenient, but you may need more space and professionalism. On the other hand, renting a space provides a more professional setting but comes with additional costs. When weighing these options, consider your business goals, budget, and personal work style.

Essential Gear and Software Investments

Now, let's focus on the gear and software you'll need. Start with a good camera, prime lenses, and essential lighting equipment. Editing software such as Adobe Photoshop or Lightroom is also necessary. While it can be tempting to invest in high-end equipment, it's important to remember that the photographer, not just the gear, makes the magic happen. Start with what you need to produce quality work and upgrade as your business grows. Budget-friendly options are available that won't break the bank but will still help you capture stunning shots.

The decisions you make while setting up your photography business, from legalities to studio setup and equipment choices, will lay the foundation for your business. Remember, the goal is to create art and build  a sustainable  business that allows you to pursue your passion for photography. Take these initial steps seriously, but don't forget to enjoy the process—it's not just a business; it's your passion turned into a profession!

# Chapter 2- Pricing Strategies for Your Photography Services

Understanding Your Market

So, you've got your camera ready, your studio set up just right, and your skills are sharper than a tack—what's next? Ah, the ever-intimidating task of setting your prices. Before you pull numbers out of thin air, let's get down to some serious business reconnaissance. Understanding your local market is like being a detective in your backyard. You're not just spying on the competition to see who's charging what but understanding why they're charging those rates. It's all about context. Are they offering quick 30-minute sessions or a full-day affair with makeup and wardrobe changes? Dive into their service lists, peek at their portfolios, and if you're feeling particularly bold, why not book a session? Experience their service and see what your future clients might expect from you.

This sleuthing gives you a benchmark. But remember, it's not just about matching or undercutting prices It's about understanding the value behind those numbers. What are clients in your area willing to pay? This might involve some trial and error coupled with feedback gathering. Surveys, informal chats post-session, and keeping an eye on how quickly (or slowly) your bookings fill up can provide invaluable insights into your market's price sensitivity. It's about finding that sweet spot where your price meets your clients' perception of your value.

Creating Pricing Packages

Now, with your detective hat still on, let's talk packages. Creating pricing packages isn't just slapping together a few services and calling it a day—it's about crafting experiences your clients can choose from, much like a menu at a fancy restaurant. Each package should cater to different needs and budgets. Start with a basic package, something that covers your essentials. Then, build up to more premium options, including additional features like extra time, more photos, special editing, or even wardrobe changes. This tiered approach caters to a broader range of clients and gently nudges customers towards higher-value options.

When constructing these packages, keep clarity in mind. Each package should clearly state what it includes, how much it costs, and what makes it different. This clarity helps clients feel informed and confident in their choices, reducing the back-and-forth that can often delay bookings. Plus, who doesn't appreciate knowing exactly what they're getting into? It's like seeing the ingredients listed on your smoothie; it feels right.

Communicating Value to Clients

Speaking of feeling right, let's talk about communicating the value of your services. This is where your inner salesperson needs to shine, not by being pushy but by being transparent and passionate about your offer. Start by highlighting what sets your photography services apart. Do you provide an unrivaled turnaround time? Are your lighting techniques straight out of a fairy tale? It could be your ability to make clients feel at ease, a not-so-minor feat in the often nerve-wracking experience of being in front of a camera. Whatever your strengths, ensure they're front and center in your conversations, website, and marketing materials.

But it's not just about what you say; it's about how you make your clients feel. Ensure that every interaction, from the initial inquiry to the final delivery, is smooth, professional, and personalized. When clients understand the effort, skill, and care that goes into creating their photographs, they're more likely to appreciate the value and less likely to quibble over price. It's about building that trust and appreciation that turns first-time clients into lifelong fans.

Adjusting Prices as Your Business Grows

Lastly, let's not forget that your pricing isn't set in stone. As your skills sharpen, your portfolio expands, and your reputation soars, your prices should reflect that growth. Reviewing your prices periodically—say, annually—allows you to adjust them to better reflect your current standing in the market. Maybe you've invested in better gear, attended a prestigious workshop, or honed your craft to near perfection. All these developments can justify a price adjustment that your clients, especially the repeat ones, will likely understand and respect.

Raising prices can be nerve-wracking, but if done thoughtfully, it can be a seamless transition. Communicate changes ahead of time and explain the reasons behind the increase. Offer grandfathering rates to existing clients or a booking window at old prices before the new ones take effect. This approach not only eases your clients into the transition but also shows that you value their loyalty, making the pill of price increase a tad sweeter to swallow.

So, there you go; from understanding your market to adjusting your prices, these strategies are about much more than just numbers. They are about building a sustainable business that respects your worth as a photographer and meets your client's needs with professionalism and care. Remember, every price tag you set reflects your confidence in your craft, so wear it proudly.

# Chapter 3- Photography Marketing 101: Tips for Photographers

Identifying Your Ideal Client

Let's find the perfect match between you and your potential clients. Identifying your ideal clients so that you can tailor your services and marketing strategies to meet their needs is essential. Whether you are interested in capturing professional shots for corporate professionals or working with the artistic community, understanding your potential clients is crucial. Consider demographics such as age, occupation, and lifestyle to customize your marketing messages and resonate with your target audience.

Developing a Marketing Plan

With your ideal client in mind, it's time to create a comprehensive marketing plan that includes both online and offline strategies. Your website should showcase your portfolio and make it easy for clients to book sessions, while social media platforms can serve as a visual gallery to attract potential clients. Additionally, email marketing keeps clients engaged and informed about your services. Regarding offline strategies, consider participating in community events, hosting workshops, and seizing every opportunity to build trust and familiarity within your local community.

## Leveraging Word-of-Mouth

Word-of-mouth is a powerful tool for growing your photography business. Encourage satisfied clients to spread the word about their positive experiences by offering a referral program and making it easy for them to share their photos on social media. Each tagged post serves as a free advertisement, directly reaching your target audience.

## Measuring Marketing Success

Utilize analytics tools to measure the effectiveness of your marketing efforts. By setting clear goals and regularly reviewing your progress, you can make informed decisions, refine your strategies to reach your ideal clients, and continuously improve your marketing game. Remember, marketing is an ongoing experiment, so be prepared to make adjustments based on the insights you gather.

# Chapter 4- Social Media and Online Presence: Building Your Brand

Choosing the Right Platforms

Navigating the bustling social media landscape is like attending a massive party and deciding who to chat with. You can only mingle with some, so you choose based on interests, vibes, and where you will most likely make meaningful connections! In the realm of photography, not all platforms are created equal when it comes to showcasing your photography expertise. With its visual-centric layout, Instagram is the belle of the ball for photographers. It's where your stunning shots can truly pop and attract immediate attention. Pinterest, too, serves as a fantastic gallery for your work, appealing particularly to those planning events or looking to update their professional portfolios.

Then there's LinkedIn, the professional networking giant. It's not just for suits and corporate speak; it's also a goldmine for photographers specializing in professional headshots. Here, you can connect directly with professionals who value and require high-quality personal branding images. The trick is to choose platforms where your target clients are already hanging out and engaging. Each platform has its language and etiquette, so once you pick your party spot, speak the lingo. Share content that resonates with the specific audience of that platform—whether it's behind-the-scenes shots on Instagram, pin-worthy editorial shots on Pinterest, or before-and-after transformations on LinkedIn.

Creating Engaging Content

Now, about making waves with your content—think of each post as a mini-story where your shots are the protagonists. The plot? Showing off your skill and versatility. Instagram loves a good narrative, so why not share the story behind a particular shoot? Talk about the challenges, the on-the-spot creative decisions, or how you brought a client's vision to life. These stories showcase your technical skills and humanize your brand, making potential clients feel connected and confident in your hands.

But let's not stop at images. Videos are like the secret sauce of social media engagement. A quick time-lapse of your editing process or a heartfelt testimonial from a satisfied client can boost your content's engagement. Also, consider live sessions or Q&As where you interact directly with your followers, answering their burning questions or giving live critiques or tutorials. This interactive content spikes engagement and builds trust and authority in your niche.

Building a Professional Website

Your website is your digital storefront, and just like any high-street shop, its layout, signage, and the goodies inside determine whether people walk in or stroll by. To convert visitors into clients, ensure your website mirrors your professionalism and artistic flair. Start with a clean, easy-to-navigate layout. No one enjoys a treasure hunt when they're just trying to view your portfolio or book a session. Speaking of portfolios, yours should be front and center—beautifully displayed with high-resolution images that load faster than you can say 'cheese.'

Include an 'About Me' section where your personality shines. People don't just buy services; they buy relationships. Let them know who you are, why you love what you do, and what makes your approach unique. And, of course, don't hide your contact information in a corner. Make it prominent with a simple, straightforward booking process. An online booking system? Even better. It's like offering your clients a VIP pass to your schedule, letting them choose their spot without back-and- forth emails.

SEO Basics for Photographers

Let's demystify SEO (Search Engine Optimization) because what good is a stunning website if no one can find it? Think of SEO as the beacon that guides clients through the vast ocean of the internet straight to your shores. Start with keyword research. Tools like Google Keyword Planner or Moz Keyword Explorer can help you understand what potential clients are searching for. Are they looking for 'professional headshot photographers,' 'family photographers' or 'product photography'? Once you know, sprinkle these keywords across your website—your titles, descriptions, and content.

But SEO isn't just about keywords. Google loves quality and relevance. Ensure your website is updated regularly with fresh content that answers your clients' questions. Start a blog where you share tips on preparing for a session or the latest trends in professional photography. Also, optimize your website's mobile version. More people than ever are browsing on their phones, and a mobile-friendly site boosts your SEO ranking significantly.

Engaging in these strategies transforms your online presence from passive to dynamic, turning your digital spaces into active tools that work tirelessly to attract and convert clients. From choosing the right platforms to optimizing your website for search engines, every step enhances your visibility and allure in the digital world. Keep your content fresh and your interactions genuine, and watch as your online presence becomes just as powerful and persuasive as your work.

# Chapter 5- Client Consultations: Winning Strategies and Common Pitfalls

Client consultations are crucial opportunities to convert inquiries into booked photography sessions. Proper preparation, building rapport, handling objections, and following up are key strategies to ensure success.

Preparing for Consultations

Preparation is essential for a successful consultation. Start by outlining the flow of the meeting, including a warm introduction, a portfolio presentation tailored to the client's needs, a discussion of services and logistics, and ending with a clear call to action.

Building Rapport

Building rapport with potential clients is vital. Actively listen to their needs, engage with their stories, and make the consultation a conversation rather than just a sales pitch.

Connecting personally with clients can make a significant difference in booking your services.

## Handling Objections

Objections are common, but they are opportunities for clarification, reassurance, and negotiation. Rather than immediately discounting prices or services, highlight the value of what you offer and suggest tailored solutions that fit within the client's needs and budget.

## Follow-up After Consultations

Follow-up is crucial after a consultation. Timely follow-ups show professionalism and dedication to client satisfaction. Additionally, timing the follow-up within 24 to 48 hours post-consultation can significantly increase booking rates. Making it easy for the client to finalize the booking in the follow-up can also lead to a positive outcome.

Mastering client consultations requires preparation, personal connection, and persistence. Each consultation is an opportunity to shine, connect genuinely, and turn potential clients into booked busy photography sessions.

# Chapter 6- Managing Client Expectations and Deliverables

Setting Clear Expectations

Imagine setting out on a photography project without a clear plan or direction. Without a clear road map, unexpected challenges could arise, and achieving your desired results would likely take longer. Managing client expectations in photography is similar to planning a successful journey. Establishing clear expectations from the outset and outlining what clients can anticipate throughout the process is crucial. This involves discussing deliverables, timelines, and post-processing details. Clarity at this stage helps to prevent misunderstandings and sets a tone of professionalism.

Begin by creating a comprehensive client welcome pack or guide that outlines each step of your photography process. Include information about what clients need to prepare, what to expect during the shoot, and what to anticipate after the session. For example, explain how many images they will receive, how they will be able to make their selection and the typical duration of the editing process. This guide will leave clients feeling well-informed and confident in their capabilities. Remember, well-informed clients are happy clients. They understand what to expect and are likelier to be pleased with the results.

Effective Communication Throughout the Project

Maintaining open communication throughout the photography project is akin to ensuring everyone is on the same page. Regular updates contribute to maintaining good client relationships. Whether it's a brief email confirming a session date, informing clients that their proofs are ready for viewing or checking in during the editing process for feedback, these gestures make clients feel valued and engaged.

Consider establishing scheduled check-ins at various project stages, especially for more significant or intricate photography assignments. This could be done via email, phone calls, or by providing clients with a personalized portal on your website where they can track the status of their projects. Tools like these keep clients informed, saving you from a barrage of 'just checking in' emails and ensuring a transparent and relatively stress-free process.

Delivering on Promises

Delivering on promises is where you have the opportunity to truly shine. Meeting deadlines, providing high-quality images, and adhering to the specifics of your client agreement all fall under this umbrella. If you promised a specific turnaround time, do everything you can to stick to that timeline. If you agree to provide a certain number of edited images, meet or exceed that number. Consistently fulfilling your promises builds trust and reliability, elevating your reputation from good to exceptional.

However, why stop at merely meeting expectations when you can exceed them? Consider providing extra edits, delivering your work earlier than expected, or including a small thank-you note or gift when returning the final images. These small gestures can turn a satisfied client into a loyal advocate for your photography business. They're the unexpected touches that can transform a pleasing photography experience into something extraordinary.

Handling Dissatisfied Clients

Despite your best efforts, there will be occasions when clients are only partially satisfied with the outcome. They may have had different expectations, or there may have been a lapse in communication. Dealing with dissatisfied clients gracefully is crucial; think of it as a test of your customer service skills. First and foremost, actively listen to their concerns. Allow them to express their thoughts without interruption. Often, simply feeling heard can alleviate their frustration and pave the way for finding a resolution.

Once you understand their concerns, consider what can be done to address the situation. Can the images be re-edited? Is a re-shoot a viable option? Provide practical solutions where possible. If dissatisfaction arises from unclear expectations from the start, consider this a learning opportunity to refine how you communicate your services and manage expectations in the future.

Maintaining professionalism is crucial, particularly in situations where a resolution could be more straightforward. Calmly explain what can and cannot be done, always emphasizing your desire to ensure their satisfaction within the boundaries of your established policies. Transforming a negative experience into a positive one can sometimes turn a disgruntled client into your most vocal supporter, demonstrating that challenges, when handled effectively, can be opportunities in disguise.

Navigating client relationships through clear expectations, open communication, and a commitment to delivering quality is more than just good business practice; it's an art form that builds your brand's reputation, one satisfied client at a time. So, continue steering with confidence and care, knowing that every interaction is a step toward establishing a resilient and respected photography business.

# Chapter 7- Navigating the Challenges of Freelance Photography

Time Management

Ah, time management—the mythical beast every photographer tries to tame! When juggling photoshoots, editing, marketing, and the never-ending administrative tasks, it can feel like you're spinning plates while riding a unicycle. But fear not; with a few clever strategies, you can keep those plates spinning without a sweat. Start by embracing the power of scheduling. Think of your daily schedule as a recipe; each ingredient needs cooking time. Allocate specific blocks of time for shooting, editing, answering emails, and even scrolling through social media. Tools like Google Calendar or Trello can be lifesavers, helping you visualize your week at a glance and adjust on the fly.

Another hot tip? Prioritize like a pro. Not all tasks are created equal. Identify your most critical actions—directly affecting your income or client satisfaction—and tackle them first. Everything else can wait. Also, don't forget to set aside time for unexpected tasks or delays. Let's face it: no day goes perfectly to plan, especially in the dynamic world of photography. A buffer period can keep you from feeling flustered when things inevitably go sideways.

Lastly, consider batching similar tasks together. Power through all your editing in one go, or set a day just for client consultations. This approach minimizes the constant mental gear-shifting that can wear you down and consume your time. By streamlining your tasks, you work more efficiently and free up chunks of time to relax or pursue personal projects, keeping the creative juices flowing without burnout.

Maintaining Work-Life Balance

Speaking of burnout, maintaining a healthy work-life balance is not just an excellent idea—it's essential for your sanity and creativity. When your home is your office, it's tempting to blur the lines between personal and work time. Who hasn't thought, "I'll just do a bit of editing before bed," only to find themselves at the computer at midnight? To avoid this, set clear boundaries, have a designated workspace, stick to defined working hours, and when the workday is done, close the door—or at least shut down the computer—and step back into your personal life.

Make sure to schedule downtime like you would a client meeting. It's that important. Engage in activities that recharge your batteries. Regular breaks prevent burnout and enhance your creativity, whether it's yoga, a movie night, or a peaceful walk. Remember, a well-rested photographer is a more productive and creative photographer.

Also, try to automate or outsource tasks that suck up your time without providing much value. Whether it's accounting, social media management, or even housekeeping, freeing up more time to focus on what you love and excel at can vastly improve your quality of life and job satisfaction. This investment in your well-being pays dividends in terms of productivity and happiness.

Dealing with Inconsistent Income

Now, onto one of the scariest parts of photography—the feast-or-famine nature of income. One month, you're the king of the world, booking back-to-back shoots; the next, you wonder if your email is broken because it's so quiet. First, it's crucial to budget wisely. During those feast periods, resist the urge to splurge. Save some of your income for leaner months, and consider diversifying your revenue streams. Maybe sell prints online, offer workshops, or venture into stock photography. Having multiple income sources can buffer against slow periods and reduce financial stress.

Another savvy move is to build an emergency fund. Aim for three to six months' worth of expenses saved up. This safety net can be a lifesaver when clients are sparse. It also allows you to be selective about your projects, ensuring you can always work on jobs that resonate with your artistic vision.

Finding Support and Resources

Last but not least, let's talk about the power of community. Photography can be isolating, but remember, you're not alone.

Connecting with other photographers through online forums, social media groups, or local meet-ups can be incredibly enriching. These connections can lead to friendships, collaborations, and learning opportunities from others' experiences. Plus, sharing your struggles and successes with people who understand what you're going through is always comforting.

Remember not to underestimate the value of mentorship, too. Finding a mentor who has navigated the photography world can provide guidance, inspiration, and practical tips tailored to your specific challenges. In return, consider mentoring someone else. Teaching can be a fantastic way to solidify your knowledge and give back to the community that supports you.

Participating in photography groups and attending workshops helps you stay up-to-date with industry trends and keeps you connected to the creative pulse of your profession. The inspiration and energy from these interactions fuel your passion and drive for photography, making the freelance journey less daunting and much more rewarding.

# Chapter 8- Legal and Ethical Considerations in Professional Photography

Navigating professional photography's legal and ethical landscape isn't just about keeping your gear in line; it's about ensuring your entire operation is straight and narrow. Think of it as a rule book that maintains fairness and integrity for everyone involved. Let's delve into this rule book, beginning with the fundamentals of copyright law. When you capture that perfect shot, you automatically hold the copyright to that image, granting you the exclusive right to decide how your photos are utilized, whether in print, online, or for sale. However, it's crucial to have evidence to support your ownership. Consider registering your photographs with the copyright office to establish clear ownership, similar to stamping a "mine" label on your work, which can be invaluable if someone decides to use your art without permission.

Contracts and model releases also play a vital role. If

copyright law is a lock for your studio, then contracts and model releases serve as security cameras. They safeguard you and your clients by outlining expectations, deliverables, and permissions. For every shoot, a contract covering everything from payment terms to image usage is essential. Model releases are equally critical, ensuring that your models consent for their images to be used commercially and protecting you against privacy claims. This is akin to seeking permission before posting a humorous photo of a friend asleep with pizza on their face—it ensures that everyone is content with the arrangement.

Ethical considerations are equally important. Respecting client privacy and accurately representing your subjects is imperative. This involves being transparent about what you can deliver and carefully handling your client's data and images. If you engage in editing, maintaining accuracy is critical—avoid altering their appearance to the extent that they are unrecognizable. It's about enhancing reality, not distorting it. Always seek permission when sharing client images in your portfolio or on social media. Put yourself in their shoes—how would you feel if someone shared your photo without asking? It's about treating your clients with the respect and professionalism they deserve.

Staying informed about legal changes is crucial. Laws and regulations about digital content, privacy, and copyright are as dynamic as the technology driving them. Keeping up-to-date isn't just good practice; it's essential for protecting yourself and your business. Subscribing to photography and legal newsletters, joining professional groups, or setting up Google alerts for terms related to photography copyright law changes can all serve as your radar system, helping you navigate and adapt to the ever-evolving legal landscape of the photography world.

By fully comprehending these legal and ethical considerations, you safeguard your business and foster trust with your clients. It illustrates that you're committed to doing things the right way, respecting both the art and the legal aspects associated with it. This dedication to integrity sets you apart in the competitive realm of photography, making you not just a skilled photographer but a reputable one. Keeping your legal obligations in order and maintaining ethical standards will help you avoid potential legal entanglements and position your business as one known for its professionalism and integrity.

# Chapter 9- Building and Presenting a Compelling Photography Portfolio

Think of your portfolio as a visual narrative, a collection of your best work that tells the story of your artistic journey. It's an opportunity to make a striking first impression, akin to the opening scene of a blockbuster film. When selecting the work for your portfolio, consider it as casting the leading roles for a movie. These images should showcase your technical prowess, creativity, and versatility. Include various photographs that demonstrate different styles, techniques, and perspectives. This variety allows potential clients to see the breadth of your skills and visualize themselves in the scenes you capture. Remember, every photo in your portfolio should serve a purpose. One image might exhibit your mastery of lighting, while another might convey a compelling and emotive story without words. Quality trumps quantity; choose your portfolio contents thoughtfully to captivate and intrigue your audience.

Tailoring your portfolio to your target audience is akin to tailoring a performance to resonate with a specific crowd—

it heightens the chance of striking a chord. Begin by understanding the preferences and needs of your ideal clients. Do they seek captivating landscapes for travel publications? Or perhaps they are in search of dynamic event photography for marketing purposes? Once you have a clear understanding, customize your portfolio to resonate with them. This could involve highlighting scenic landscapes for travel companies or showcasing vibrant and energetic event photography for corporate clients. Consider creating distinct sections or separate portfolios for different niche markets. This targeted approach demonstrates to potential clients that you comprehend their specific needs and possess the expertise to fulfill them.

In the digital era, the presentation of your portfolio is just as crucial as its content. Online portfolios offer convenience and accessibility, meeting the expectations of today's clients. They ensure that your work is just a click away from potential clients across the globe. Ensure that your online portfolio is user- friendly, loads swiftly, and displays elegantly on all devices. High-quality images and a polished, professional design mirror the caliber of your work. However, there is also immense value in a physical portfolio. There is an undeniable impact in presenting a beautifully printed photograph. Engaging the sense of touch adds a layer of sophistication and seriousness to your presentation. Physical portfolios can be particularly effective in face-to-face meetings, where the tactile quality of the prints can make a powerful and enduring statement. The key is to leverage online and physical portfolios to your advantage, ensuring they complement each other and cater to different viewing preferences.

Regularly updating your portfolio is crucial to maintaining its relevance and appeal. Your portfolio should follow suit as your skills grow and your style evolves. Periodically revisiting and revising your collection ensures that it accurately reflects your current abilities and artistic direction. This might involve bidding farewell to older works that no longer represent your best or are no longer aligned with your current style. It also means adding fresh content that showcases new techniques you've mastered and new experiences you've gained. An up-dated portfolio demonstrates your growth and dedication to your craft, keeping your presentation fresh and engaging for returning visitors. It showcases that you are active, evolving, and continuously expanding the horizons of your art.

As you craft and refine your portfolio, remember that it's more than just a compilation of images. It embodies your unique vision and skills, serves as a means to connect with potential clients, and acts as a gateway to new opportunities. Invest the time and thought it deserves, and watch as it unlocks doors to new possibilities and paths in your photography career.

# Chapter 10- Expanding Your Network: Collaborations and Community Engagement

Let's discuss spreading your creative wings and diving into the big, beautiful world of networking and collaboration. Now, I know what you might think—networking sounds as fun as organizing your tax receipts. But trust me, with a pinch of strategy and a dash of your natural charm, it can be as rewarding as nailing that perfect shot on a challenging day. So, why network? Well, connecting with fellow photographers and other creatives isn't just about swapping business cards and following each other on Instagram. It's about building a community that supports, inspires, and drives everyone forward. Imagine creating your creative eco-system, where everyone brings something unique.

Engaging with other photographers, especially those who might share your niche, can open up a treasure trove of opportunities. From co-hosting workshops that showcase your collective skills to sharing gigs when your schedule is overflowing, the benefits are as plentiful as SD cards at a busy event. But here's the real kicker—referrals. Yes, in an industry where trust is king, having a network of peers who trust your work enough to recommend you to their clients can be golden. It's like having a team of unofficial marketing agents, all because you took the time to build genuine connections.

And speaking of connections, let's pay attention to the magic of collaborating with makeup artists and stylists. These artists are not just about making people look good; they're about enhancing the visual storytelling in your photographs. Imagine this: you're set to shoot a portrait session. Pretty standard stuff, right? But add a stylist into the mix, and suddenly, your subject's attire is as striking as your photography skills. Bring a makeup artist into the session, and those minor imperfections disappear, not in post-production, but right there during the shoot. The result? Portraits that are polished and professional make your subject shine and, by extension, make your portfolio shine even brighter.

But let's take this beyond the studio lights and into the heart of your local community. Engaging with your community might sound daunting, but it's about connecting with the world outside your door. Participate in local events, offer to shoot at community gatherings, or hold a mini-exhibit at your local cafe showcasing your work. Each activity increases your visibility and roots you as a vital part of the community fabric. People start recognizing your face, not just your photographs, and in a business where familiarity breeds trust, this can lead to a steady stream of clients who feel a personal connection to you.

Lastly, immerse yourself in photography groups and online forums. Yes, the digital realm is teeming with communities that span the globe. These platforms are about sharing your latest shots and learning, sharing, and growing together. Do you have a lighting dilemma? Throw it into a forum. Chances are someone has been there and figured it out. Want feedback on a new editing technique? Post it in a group and watch the constructive critiques roll in. These interactions, while virtual, can significantly impact your real-world skills and knowledge. Plus, they keep you on your toes, pushing you to stay current and competitive in an ever-evolving industry.

So there you have it. Networking and collaboration might seem like just another to-do on your ever-growing list, but they are indispensable tools in your photography toolkit. They open doors to new opportunities and learning and enrich your professional journey, making it a shared adventure rather than a solitary slog. So step out, reach out, and watch as your network becomes your net worth in more ways than one.

# Chapter 11- Staying Creative and Inspired: Continuing Your Photographic Journey

Continuing Education

There's a little secret in the photography world that keeps the best snapping stunning shots, year after year—never stop learning. It's tempting to rest on your laurels once you've mastered the exposure triangle or nailed your post-processing workflow, but let's face it: the realm of photography is as dynamic as a flashbulb. Diving into ongoing education is a must to keep your skills as sharp as your lenses. Workshops can open your eyes to new techniques and trends, whether in-person or online. Picture yourself in a workshop learning the latest in lighting technology or a new method of post-editing that might revolutionize your workflow. These learning experiences are skill enhancers and great venues to rub shoulders with peers and mentors who can offer fresh perspectives and insights.

Online courses and tutorials offer a buffet of learning opportunities at your fingertips, often available on-demand to suit your hectic schedule. Platforms like Udemy, Coursera, or even specific photography-focused sites offer courses ranging from the basics to advanced niche-specific skills. But don't just watch—practice. Apply these new skills in simulated setups or shoots to transform theoretical knowledge into practical prowess. And let's not forget the wealth of books and magazines out there. Sometimes, flipping through the pages of a well- crafted photography book can spark that creative flame as effectively as any high-tech workshop.

Personal Projects

Personal projects can be your creative oasis if you feel the creative burnout from all those client shoots. These projects are your playground. They're where you can experiment without constraints, try out bizarre compositions, play with unconven- tional lighting, or dive into a photography genre you've never tried before. It could be a documentary project on the life of urban street performers or a surreal portrait series inspired by your favorite sci-fi movies. These personal endeavors push the boundaries of your creativity, challenging you to think and shoot outside your comfort zone.

The beauty of personal projects lies in their ability to reignite your passion for photography. They remind you why you picked up a camera in the first place—not just to pay the bills but to capture the world through your unique lens. Plus, these projects can unexpectedly open new doors. Sharing this work on social media or photography exhibitions can attract attention from potential clients who might be drawn to your work's style and emotional depth, leading to new professional opportunities.

## Seeking Inspiration

Inspiration fuels creativity; luckily, it's scattered generously throughout the world. For photographers, inspiration can come from a myriad of sources. Art's diverse forms and expressions can spark new ideas for poses, compositions, or themes. Visit galleries or dive into art books and observe how artists use color, light, and form. Cinema, another rich source, offers a visual feast of framing, lighting, and character portrayal that can translate beautifully into portrait photography. Watch films critically, noting how cinematographers compose shots and directors elicit emotions, then bring those cinematic techniques into your photography.

Fashion, too, influences portrait photography profoundly. The play of fabrics, the evolution of styles, and the boldness of runway shows can inspire fresh approaches to how you dress and style your subjects. Follow fashion blogs, watch emerging designers, or even collaborate with a fashion stylist to bring a couture edge to your shots. And don't overlook the everyday — sometimes, the most powerful inspiration comes from the people and places in your daily life. A smile from a stranger, the atmosphere of a café, or the chaos of a city street could spark the concept for your next big project.

## Adapting and Evolving

In a field as dynamic as photography, adaptability is critical. The tools, technologies, and trends are constantly changing, and keeping pace can be the difference between staying relevant and becoming obsolete. Embrace change, whether upgrading to the latest camera gear to enhance image quality or adopting new software to streamline your workflow. But it's not just about gear and gadgets; it's also about adapting your business strategies and marketing efforts to align with changing market conditions and client expectations.

Stay flexible in your business plans, ready to pivot when a particular strategy doesn't pan out or when a new opportunity presents itself. It's shifting more business online in response to global changes or tapping into a new market segment that suddenly shows potential. Keep your ear to the ground, listen to client feedback, and stay attuned to industry trends. This proactive approach ensures that your photography business survives and thrives, no matter what challenges or changes the market throws your way.

As you continue on this exciting photographic journey, remem- ber that staying creative and inspired is not a passive process. It requires action—learning, experimenting, seeking out new sources of inspiration, and being willing to change and evolve. This active pursuit of growth and inspiration will keep your passion for photography vibrant and your career in photography dynamic and fulfilling.

As we wrap up this chapter on staying creatively charged and inspired, remember a photographer's journey is one of constant discovery and re-invention. Each image you capture is not just a reflection of your subject but of your journey as an artist and a professional.

# Conclusion

Reflecting on our adventure, it's clear that photography is much more than just snapping pictures. It's about mastering the dance of light and shadows, learning the delicate art of directing and posing to capture the very soul of your subjects, and refining those captures into polished gems through post-processing. And let's remember the grand finale of knitting all these skills into the fabric of a successful photography business.

But here's the kicker—whether you're aiming to become the next big name in photography or just looking to seriously upgrade your Instagram game, the skills and insights we've shared are universal. They don't discriminate based on your fancy equipment or background; they're about your passion and dedication to the craft.

So, what's next on your photographic horizon? I urge you not to let this be the end. The world of photography is as vast as it is dynamic. Keep exploring, keep learning. New techniques, styles, and technologies are popping up faster than you can say "cheese." Experiment fearlessly because every mistake is just a lesson in disguise, and every triumph is a story waiting to be told.

And speaking of stories, remember that your work can do more than fill space on a hard drive. You're capturing moments, personalities, and potential. Each shot could be the key to someone's dream job, a cherished memory for a family, or a memento of a life milestone. That's a magical ability, so wield it with pride and care.

I can't send you off without a massive thank you for picking up this book and walking this path with me. Sharing these insights has been as rewarding for you as for me. But our journey doesn't have to end here. I invite you to keep the conversation going— share your work, highs and lows, and victories. Reach out with feedback, or better yet, share your success stories. Let's keep this community thriving, learning from each other and drawing inspiration from every snapshot shared.

Now, armed with the knowledge to master your craft and the insights to build a successful business, go out there and capture the world, one incredible shot at a time. Your photography journey has just begun, and with each click of the shutter, you can make every shot count and create a thriving photography business. Reflecting on our adventure, it's clear that photography is much more than just snapping pictures. It's about mastering the dance of light and shadows, learning the delicate art of directing and posing to capture the very soul of your subjects, and refining those captures into polished gems through post-processing. And let's remember the grand finale of knitting all these skills into the fabric of a successful photography business.

But here's the kicker—whether you're aiming to become the next big name in photography or just looking to seriously upgrade your Instagram game, the skills and insights we've shared are universal. They don't discriminate based on your fancy equipment or background; they're about your passion and dedication to the craft.

So, what's next on your photographic horizon? I urge you not to let this be the end. The world of photography is as vast as it is dynamic. Keep exploring, keep learning. New techniques, styles, and technologies are popping up faster than you can say "cheese." Experiment fearlessly because every mistake is just a lesson in disguise, and every triumph is a story waiting to be told.

And speaking of stories, remember that your work can do more than fill space on a hard drive. You're capturing moments, personalities, and potential. Each shot could be the key to someone's dream job, a cherished memory for a family, or a memento of a life milestone. That's a magical ability, so wield it with pride and care.

I can't send you off without a massive thank you for picking up this book and walking this path with me. Sharing these insights has been as rewarding for you as for me. But our journey doesn't have to end here. I invite you to keep the conversation going— share your work, highs and lows, and victories. Reach out with feedback, or better yet, share your success stories. Let's keep this community thriving, learning from each other and drawing inspiration from every snapshot shared.

Now, armed with the knowledge to master your craft and the insights to build a successful business, go out there and capture the world, one incredible shot at a time. Your photography journey has just begun, and with each click of the shutter, you can make every shot count and create a thriving photography business.

# Also by Amanda Otis

This photography book series is your ultimate resource for mastering the art and business of photography. Each book is packed with expert insights, practical advice, and inspiring examples to help you grow your skills and succeed in the competitive world of photography. Whether you're just starting out or looking to refine your craft, these guides will support you every step of the way on your photographic journey.

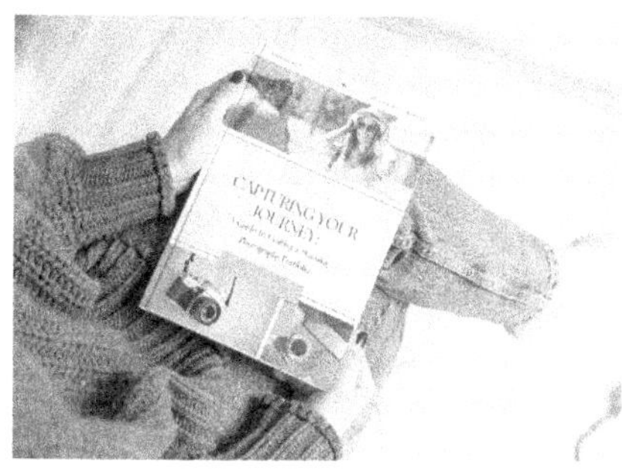

Capturing Your Journey: A Guide to Crafting a Stunning Photography Portfolio (with Helpful Worksheets and 50 Portfolio Building Exercises)

Embark on a transformative journey through the lens with "Capturing Your Journey," a comprehensive guided workbook

designed for photographers aspiring to build their perfect port- folio. This 26-page workbook is a treasure trove of portfolio- building insights, offering a wealth of information and 50 dynamic exercises tailored to help you curate a portfolio that reflects your unique style and vision.

Discover the art of thematic thinking, find your passion, develop depth in your work, and master the art of tight editing with practical exercises that guide you every step of the way. Whether you're a budding photographer or a seasoned pro, this workbook is your companion in honing your craft and creating a portfolio that stands out.

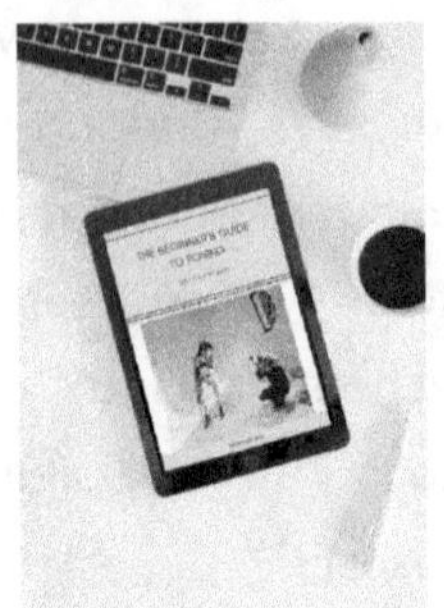

**The Beginner's Guide to Posing (with Pictures!)**
https://otisdesignboutique.etsy.com/
listing/1640479201

This ebook takes your posing game to the next level. Whether you're a seasoned model or a selfie enthusiast, this guide is your go-to resource for striking the perfect pose every time.

What's Inside:

A curated collection of 17 pages featuring various poses suitable for any occasion. From casual to sophisticated, these poses are designed to make you look your best. Visualize each pose with stunning images that showcase the art of posing.

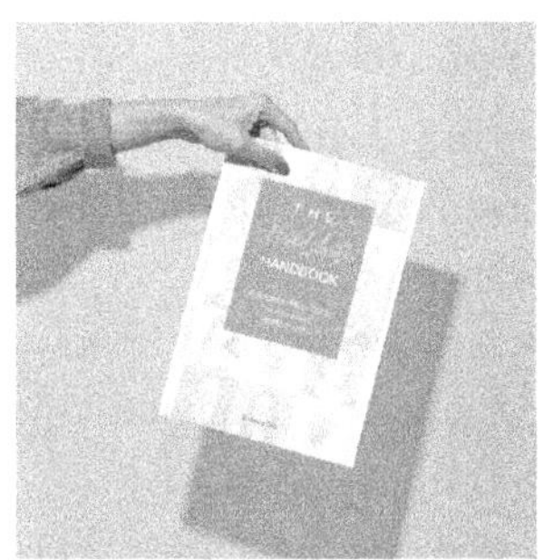

### The Headshot Handbook: A Step-by-Step Guide to Headshot Photography

Unlock the secrets to capturing stunning headshots with "The Headshot Handbook: A Step-by- Step Guide to Headshot Photogra- phy." Whether you are a budding photographer or a seasoned professional looking to refine your skills, this comprehensive guide will take you through every aspect of headshot photography.

Inside, you'll find expert advice on selecting the right equipment, mastering lighting techniques, and understanding the importance of angles and expressions. Learn how to create a comfortable environment for your subjects, enabling them to convey their best selves in every shot. The book has practical tips, step-by-step tutorials, and inspiring examples to elevate your photography game.

From corporate professionals to actors and models, "The Headshot Handbook" covers diverse styles and approaches, ensuring you can meet any client's needs. Discover how to perfectly retouch and edit your photos, delivering high-quality results that stand out in today's competitive market.

Transform your headshot photography with this indispensable resource and capture images that leave a lasting impression.

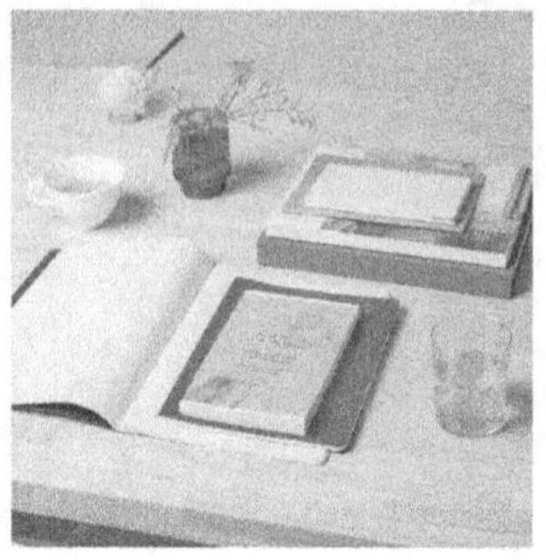

## What Do I Do With My Hands?
## : From Awkward to Awesome |
## A Photographer's Guide to Hand Posing

The subtle art of hand posing can define your photographs, transforming a simple portrait into a powerful story. It can elevate your images from simply pleasing to the eye to emotionally engaging, allowing your subjects' personalities to shine through.

But mastering hand posing is no small feat. It requires an understanding of balance, dynamics, and, most of all, storytelling.

Now, imagine having a guide that bridges the gap between theory and practice, equipping you to master hand posing in a diverse range of photographic styles. A guide that goes deeper, transforming intimidating technical details into approachable, actionable insights.

Introducing "What Do I Do With My Hands?: A Photographer's Guide to Hand Posing" — a comprehensive resource designed to help photographers master hand posing in portraits.

Every page is meant to elevate your photography and your understanding of hand posing. You'll learn not just the technical aspects of photography but also the thinking and broader perspectives of experienced photographers. So you get comprehensive coverage of the subject without overwhelming technical jargon, making it perfect for photographers at every skill level.